M000210361

THE
FORGOTTEN
SECRET
TO
PHENOMENAL
SUCCESS

Pelican Books by Mike Hernacki

THE SECRET TO CONQUERING FEAR

THE FORGOTTEN SECRET TO PHENOMENAL SUCCESS

THE
FORGOTTEN
SECRET
TO
PHENOMENAL
SUCCESS

MIKE HERNACKI

PELICAN PUBLISHING COMPANY
Gretna 1998

Published by the Berkley Publishing Group, 1992
Published by arrangement with the author by
  Pelican Publishing Company, Inc., 1998

First Pelican edition, February 1998

Library of Congress Cataloging-in-Publication Data

Hernacki, Mike.
    The forgotten secret to phenomenal success / Mike Hernacki. — 1st Pelican ed.
        p.   cm.
    Originally published: New York : Berkley Pub. Group, 1992.
    ISBN 1-56554-319-X (pbk. : alk. paper)
    1. Success.   I. Title.
BJ1611.H444   1997
158.1—DC21
                                                              97-30357
                                                              CIP

Manufactured in the United States of America
Published by Pelican Publishing Company, Inc.
P.O. Box 3110, Gretna, Louisiana 70054-3110

TO WANDA

Contents

THE
FORGOTTEN
SECRET
TO
PHENOMENAL
SUCCESS

⇒ **1**

The Most Phenomenal
Success Mechanism
on Earth

*"Success . . . means the oppor-
tunity to experience . . . to the
maximum the forces that are
within us."*
—David Sarnoff

What does success mean to you?

Maybe you define success by your *achievements*: earning a degree, getting a promotion, building a house, raising a family, finding spiritual enlightenment, climbing a mountain, winning a medal.

Or you measure success by your *possessions*: the money you earn, the car you drive, the clothes you wear, the real estate you own, the contents of your safe deposit box.

Or you find success in your *relationships*: a marriage that works, a long list of friends, an address book full of important contacts, children who love you, people who like to be on your team—at work or at play.

Maybe to you, success includes a few items from each list. Or maybe it means something nobody else would ever dream of.

The first thing to understand about success is that no matter what your definition of it may be, no matter what shape it takes, no matter how you measure it, it's all the same. Whether you're building a house, a portfolio, or a relationship, the same principles apply. The unwritten rules that govern your rise to success in your career also determine how well you'll raise your kids.

The various skills you'll need, the specific techniques you'll have to learn, the processes you'll have to go through—all these will differ from one situation to the next. But the same set of success principles applies everywhere, to everyone. And that's good, because it means that as soon as you learn that one set of principles, you're on your way.

Though we've probably never met, I'm going to tell you a few things about yourself.

TRUTH #1: You've experienced success in your life, but there are still some things you haven't achieved, and would like to.

TRUTH #2: In the past, you wanted something very much, but for one reason or another, you didn't try or you stopped trying to get it.

TRUTH #3: Somewhere along the way, you

were told there are certain things you just cannot do and certain goals you'll never achieve—and you've come to accept this.

The book you're reading contains a Secret—a marvelous Secret that can dramatically improve your record of success in the future. Whether you see yourself now as a success or a failure, you can benefit from the Secret. Whether you see yourself as capable or inept, the Secret can help. Whether you believe in it or not, the Secret can work.

The best part about this Secret is—you already know it. In fact, you've already used it, many times, to attain successes that can truly be described as phenomenal. But if any of the three truths listed above apply to you (and you know they do), then you've forgotten the Secret. I'm writing this book for one reason: to remind you of it; to bring the Forgotten Secret back into your consciousness. Naturally, what you do with it is up to you. But realize this—what you do with it will determine how successful you'll be in the future.

For the moment, don't concern yourself about what you have to do. Just being reminded of the Forgotten Secret will bring you many benefits. Just reading about it will start you on your way. As of right now, you've already begun.

Your Heritage of Success

Imagine, if you can, finding yourself in a position where you want something that's extremely difficult to achieve. You've never done it before, and have no idea how to go about it. Just getting started is an iffy proposition, and once you do, you'll have plenty of troubles. You'll have to endure months of physical stress in a new and unfamiliar environment, be exposed to any number of traumas and trials, then undertake a hazardous journey in order to reach your goal.

Can you do it? Can you overcome such tremendous hardship? Can you succeed in a situation as "impossible" as this?

The answer is yes, because you've already done it. And the story of how you did it is nothing short of phenomenal.

To relive the story of your success, we have to go back to the very beginning—*your* beginning. You began your life as a tiny, helpless organism, growing in your mother's womb. From the first moments of your existence, it was not in your nature to be hesitant or intimidated. You had no insecurities or self-doubts. You were driven by a built-in success mechanism that was just beginning to serve you.

Instinctively, you became larger and stronger. You survived and progressed, even though you were subjected to some awful treatment. It's possible your mother smoked cigarettes, thereby contracting her blood vessels and choking off the oxygen you needed so desperately. Maybe your mother drank alcohol. After all, only since the mid-1980s have women come to know just how much harm they can cause by drinking while pregnant. Maybe your mother took drugs—for medical treatment or for pleasure—not knowing the trauma she was causing to your tiny system. Maybe she was in an accident and you were jammed hard against the steering wheel of her car. Maybe she missed catching a softball and you got beaned. Or maybe she worked hard and was tired all the time.

Yet you survived. You grew. You developed. Then, after months of this difficulty, you undertook a journey that, despite medical advances, still claims the lives of millions of babies every year. But you were born, probably kicking and screaming. The most powerful success mechanism on earth had done its work. And even that was only another beginning. You then went on to score a series of successes that without exaggeration can be characterized as astounding.

In about a year, you learned how to walk. Therapists tell us the process of walking is so complicated, it's almost impossible to explain in words, or to teach without demonstrating. Yet you learned it, without anyone actually showing you how, and with only occasional encouragement from adults.

Within two years of being born, you learned to talk. By the time you were four or five, you had mastered about 90 percent of the words and phrases you would use regularly throughout the rest of your life. If you were raised in a bilingual household, as I was, you mastered two languages in the same time span, with the same ease. Amazingly, you learned all this without books or classes or trained language teachers.

At age six or seven you tackled what educators agree is the hardest learning task a human being can undertake. You began learning how to read, and within a few short months, you had the essential skills down pat. You have used those same skills ever since, to learn just about everything you know today.

Success Is What You Are

With all these incredible accomplishments, you proved that you not only *have* a success mechanism, you *are* a success mechanism. Your ability and drive to succeed are as much a part of you as the genes that determine the color of your eyes.

The success you attained from the very first moments of your existence is part of your makeup, and comes to you as naturally as breathing. The success you enjoyed early in life flowed out of principles you understood *instinctively*. The results you achieved were brought about by behaviors you used *instinctively*. No one taught you how to succeed. When you got here, you already knew.

Sometime between then and now, you forgot those principles. You stopped using the success skills you were born with, and you lost them. That's sad, but it's not hopeless.

It's not hopeless because right now you can be reminded of those principles. You can relearn those behaviors. Right now, you can begin again to achieve successes as phenomenal as anything you've ever done before.

Remembering and relearning are not as difficult as they may seem. The mechanism is already in place. It's still a part of you. It never went away. The tremendous drive that enabled you to survive the first challenges of your life is as strong as ever.

And here's the best part. If you reacquaint yourself with the principles of achievement, if you relearn the behaviors that bring results, if you recall the Forgotten Secret, your phenomenal success is inevitable. You *will* do it.

Because success isn't just what you accomplish. Success is what you *are*.

$\Rightarrow$ **2**

The Mechanism "Forgets"

*Men are not prisoners of fate,
but only prisoners of their own
minds.*
—Franklin Delano Roosevelt

Marvelous as it is, the success mechanism that enabled you to accomplish so many great things is also vulnerable. It can be stifled, sidetracked, and reprogrammed. It can even be made to look as if it's not working at all. If you've ever fallen far short of accomplishing something you once dreamed of, chances are your success mechanism has been sabotaged along the way. If so, you're not alone. Millions of others have been undermined too. Millions have had their mechanisms tinkered with. Now they avoid, and even dread, success.

The Great Success Saboteur

Believe it or not, one of the great saboteurs of the success mechanism is an institution that supposedly exists to help people succeed: the school system. Here's how that has happened.

The modern educational system was developed nearly 150 years ago, shortly after the Industrial Revolution began. At the time, the rapidly growing industrial machine had a need for large numbers of workers with limited knowledge and a few usable skills. The basic premise was that a teacher, who was the custodian of knowledge, should try to pound that knowledge into the heads of children who were believed to be lazy, unmotivated, and not too bright. The teacher's job was to impart only as much knowledge and develop only as many skills as these lesser beings would need to get themselves the dead-end jobs that would feed them for the rest of their lives. The whole system was based on negative self-concepts, with heavy emphasis on regimentation and control. In the rigid discipline of the classroom, precocious behavior (often a sign of an exceptional mind) was punished. As for creativity, well, the system just had no way to deal with it.

The system had major flaws, but it did work. It did turn out lots of young people with limited knowledge and a few useful skills. It also succeeded in getting students to forget that their potential was naturally unlimited. It succeeded in tying down people's natural learning abilities and chaining their minds to the idea that they could not learn very well.

Of course, there have been many marvelous advances in education in the last century and a half. When I was studying to be an elementary school teacher in the early 1960s, I learned much about creativity, motivation, and dealing with the exceptional student. Interestingly, though, I acquired much of this information in large lecture halls, where an instructor on an elevated podium dictated the material to rows and rows of quiet, well-behaved young people who were taking "good notes" for fear of flunking the exam. Those instructors were using an old, inefficient method to teach us about the new, improved methods! Even so, as young teachers, we implemented these ideas, and the system did change.

Today's elementary school classrooms are vastly different from the "learning factories" of the nineteenth century. Discipline isn't nearly as rigid. Children are encouraged to explore and create. The emphasis has turned away from rote learning. Now the stress is on critical thinking and problem-solving.

But old ideas die hard. The late futurist Buckminster Fuller once observed that the conventional education system is at least half a century behind what science currently knows. To a large extent, that remains true today.

The system is still heavily structured into grades and levels. The learning process still mainly consists of teachers talking and students listening. And "fitting in" is still considered much more important than standing out.

The Reprogramming of Young Minds

Yes, you started life as an incredible success mechanism. You delighted everyone with how much and how fast you learned. But soon your mind, like the minds of so many others, began to be reprogrammed.

This reprogramming begins when children are quite young and continues throughout their developing years. Usually, the culprits are well-meaning parents and teachers who do the most harm while guided by the best intentions. Let me cite a few examples from my own experience. Maybe something like this even happened to you.

1. The Second-Rate Sibling. When I was in grade school, I had a little friend who was simply brilliant. Jimmy read books most of us had never heard of; he played chess; and for fun, he solved mathematical puzzles. Trouble was, he had an older brother of just average intelligence. From the time Jimmy was old enough to talk, his parents told him not to "show off his brains," because it would hurt his brother's feelings. When he got dazzling grades, he was ignored. When he won a spelling bee, it was hushed up. Only when his performance was mediocre did he get a slap on the back.

Eventually, Jimmy's need for love and approval overcame his need to succeed. He began to settle for B's and C's; he played baseball (poorly) rather than chess, and he lost interest in math. Ultimately, he became a discipline problem and was expelled from our school, so I lost track of him.

2. The "Problem Daughter." A variation of Situation #1 occurs when girls are more capable than boys. Although I went to an all-boys high school, I was friends with a girl at another school who was a classic overachiever. Karen did practically everything better than anyone else, including the boys. She even excelled in sports, which in those days were almost entirely the boys' bailiwick, and which girls participated in only for "physical education," not achievement.

Karen got high praise from some of her teachers (especially the females), but her parents and friends constantly warned her that "showing up the boys" would make her unpopular and she would wind up "an old maid." Like my little friend in grade school, she too learned to hide her abilities, trading excellence for acceptance. At high school graduation, she was the salutatorian, meaning she was number two in overall grade point average. The valedictorian was a boy. I knew him too, and he wasn't nearly as smart as she.

3. The Infallible IQ Test. Speaking of intelligent girls, all through grade school and most of high school, my wife earned straight A's. When she was in the tenth grade, some university students came to her school to verify an intelligence test their professor was developing. Wanda, along with the rest of her class, took an unproven test that was supposed to measure how smart she was. A few weeks later, one of her teachers ominously called Wanda in for a private conference.

"I'm concerned that you've been cheating in school," the nun said. "According to this IQ test, you have only average intelligence. Yet your grades are so high, there's no way you could be getting them on your own. You must be cheating."

Such a dire pronouncement from so powerful an authority figure had a devastating effect on fifteen-year-old Wanda. She concluded the nun must be right. She must have average intelligence, and though she knew she hadn't been cheating, she assumed she must have been lucky over the years, and now, her luck had finally run out. For the rest of high school and college, Wanda got average or slightly above average grades. It wasn't until many years later, when she went to a difficult graduate school and got straight A's again, that Wanda realized the IQ test had been wrong, and she was naturally smart.

4. The Wrong Side of the Tracks. Wanda and I have a friend named Carla, a Mexican immigrant who married a man from the poorest part of Los Angeles. Miguel was also of Mexican descent, though he had been born and raised in the United States. For Carla, coming to America was a marvelous opportunity to succeed and prosper, so she worked hard and began raising the children she and Miguel had. But where Carla saw opportunity, Miguel saw only dead ends.

They moved to San Diego and settled in a neighborhood that was just as poverty-stricken as the one they'd left in L.A.—even though they both had jobs and could have afforded better. Whenever Carla mentioned moving to a nicer neighborhood, Miguel's response was, "That place is for rich people. Our kind can never live there." Whenever she talked of their children going to college and getting white-collar jobs, Miguel would say, "We could never afford it, so why try?"

Carla and Miguel's children never did try

very hard. Their son passed up a chance to go to community college and instead worked as a janitor—until he got into trouble with drugs and ran off to Mexico. Their daughter had a baby when she was fifteen. Though she is extraordinarily intelligent and would have qualified for several kinds of financial assistance if she had gone on with school, she stopped when she got her high school diploma and took a job in a fast-food restaurant.

In every one of these situations, someone told a miraculously gifted young person that he or she couldn't or shouldn't succeed. The person who did this was someone who had become convinced that success beyond a certain point was not possible, or at least not desirable. Ironically, this person actually meant well, hoping to save the young person from the trauma of rejection or failure.

This has happened to you; it's happened to me. We've been told, over and over again, to accept our limitations, to not reach too high, to set "realistic" goals, to be satisfied with less, and to not set ourselves up for a hard fall. Those who told us these things were people we believed and trusted. People who only wanted the best for us. All the while, our amazing success mechanism was getting rusty. Eventually, we forgot how to use it altogether.

Fear of Failure, Fear of Success

Oscar Wilde once wrote, "In this world there are only two tragedies. One is not getting what one wants and the other is getting it." Though he may have been only half-serious, Wilde hit upon what is a devastatingly widespread notion: that success is as undesirable as failure. Given how old and well-accepted this notion is, we shouldn't be surprised so many people live out their lives avoiding success rather than pursuing it.

There are any number of theories as to why people fear something that can be so beneficial to them. In *Overcoming the Fear of Success*, Martha Friedman concludes, "The fear of success is not getting what you really want because you unconsciously feel you don't deserve it." It's a paradox, she says, because consciously, no one's afraid of success. Unconsciously, though, it's a different story. Deep down, you harbor a feeling of unworthiness.

Yes, but how did that unconscious feeling *get* there? You certainly started out in life feeling you deserved anything you could get your curious little hands on.

A while back, it was believed that *motivation* controlled the success mechanism. Some psychologists theorized that the motive to avoid success arose when someone saw success as having negative consequences, such as social rejection or (in the case of women who were studious) loss of femininity. Later studies suggested that success avoidance is a *learned* response to situations in which other people let us know that the success we seek is socially unacceptable.

In 1989, Michael E. Hyland of the Department of Psychology at Plymouth Polytechnic in Plymouth, England, proposed the hypothesis that success-avoidance is actually a *compromise*. It's the result of a conflict between two contradictory goals. The goal of "getting ahead," for example, may conflict with the goal of "getting along" with people. And getting along can be a powerful objective. "If you want to get along," said the consummate politician Sam Rayburn, "go along." By that, of course, he meant *compromise*.

Faced with such a conflict between goals, a person has to choose one over the other. And it may just happen that in order to achieve one goal, the person has to behave in a way that causes them not to achieve the other.

When you and I engage in success-avoiding behavior, it's not necessarily because we fear success, or because we feel we don't deserve it, or because we think it's socially unacceptable. More likely, *it's because there's something else we want more than success*—and that "something" causes us to behave in a way that will produce failure.

If this theory is correct, the behavior that results in a "failure" is actually our way of successfully achieving a different goal. When you avoid success, you've simply decided *not* to select a goal someone else thinks is important. Instead, you've selected a goal *you* think is important. So even when you appear to be avoiding success, you're actually getting exactly what you want. In other words, you're succeeding. Your phenomenal success mechanism is so strong, it works all the time. It doesn't really "forget" how to function. In fact, it gets you exactly what you want, even when what you want is to avoid the things you and everyone else agree constitute "success."

The problem is, when you choose one kind of success over another, you don't always select what's best for you—and you often don't even know why.

If you're now working for low pay in a job you hate, you *chose* it. In fact, you choose it again and again every working day. Why? I don't know, and I suspect you don't either. Maybe you're afraid of something you think comes with a better-paying, more satisfying job. Maybe you're afraid your friends and family will reject you. Maybe, as Martha Friedman says, you unconsciously feel you don't deserve to make more money and be happy in your work. She notes that we're all struggling with a cultural paradox. It's important to win, society tells us, but it's all right, even virtuous, to lose. Unconsciously, we carry that paradox around with us.

Because so much of this "success stuff" is unconscious, people find it very hard to deal with. That may be discouraging, but it shouldn't be enough to stop you. Remember, you possess the most powerful success mechanism on earth. In the past, it's survived a lot rougher treatment than you've subjected it to lately, and it's always come through for you. Even your "failures" have actually been successes by a different name, on a different level, in a different way.

All this book is suggesting is that you start using your success mechanism consciously again. When you do, maybe you'll start to see why you've been unconsciously sabotaging yourself. Maybe you'll see that all the undesirable things you thought success would bring are actually quite nice. And maybe you'll find *this* kind of success so much more rewarding than the other kind (the one called "failure"), you'll start going after it more regularly.

Be advised, however, that you may never find out why you've been sabotaging yourself. You may never learn what's at the bottom of your "fear of success." Maybe all you'll ever learn is that success is enjoyable, rewarding, and worth every bit of the effort.

For my money, that's reason enough to pursue the Forgotten Secret. How about you?

⇒ **3**

Stumbling,
Falling,
and Getting Up

As I grow older, I pay less atten-
tion to what men say. I just
watch what they do.
                    —Andrew Carnegie

As you were approaching your first birthday, you were overcome by a powerful urge to stand upright and walk. Obeying that urge, you grabbed onto furniture, or your father's pant leg, or the family dog— anything you could use to pull yourself up. In time, you taught yourself to stand and hold onto things, then to move your feet while standing, and finally to move your feet while not holding onto anything.

Between the time you first felt the urge to walk and the time you finally took those tiny, tentative steps, you fell down thousands of times. You banged your rump on the kitchen floor. You knocked your head against tables, chairs, and cabinets. You hurt yourself and you cried, again and again.

Yet your drive to succeed was so strong, you kept on trying—with no thought of quitting, with not a moment of self-doubt—until you taught yourself to walk.

Today, you don't approach things that way. As we saw in the last chapter, you've been reprogrammed to doubt your abilities, to question your motives, and to replace someone else's objectives for your own. You've been taught to limit the number of times you'll try something, and to rationalize it when those limited attempts don't produce results. You've chosen to behave in ways that actually prevent you from getting what you want—so you can get something less desirable, even though you have no idea why.

You've learned how to procrastinate. You've learned how to make excuses. And you've learned how to quit.

Still, you get things done. Despite all your fears and doubts, you'll sometimes try something new, or dangerous, or potentially rewarding. The drive that impelled you to walk even though you'd failed thousands of times is so strong, you defy your negative programming and strive to succeed anyway.

You are not alone; all the things I just said about you are true of practically everyone. We all have learned to fail. We all are driven to succeed.

As Martha Friedman says, it's a fascinating paradox. On the one hand, we're sabotaging our success. On the other, we're pursuing our success, though in a haphazard and inefficient way. If we're going to rediscover the Forgotten Secret, we'll need to take a closer look at this paradox—and maybe learn something about ourselves in the process.

How We Sabotage Our Own Success

At first, well-meaning parents and teachers were the ones who sabotaged our success. But after a while, being excellent students, we learned how to do it ourselves.

In his book, *The Sabotage Factor,* psychiatrist Daniel G. Amen says we all sabotage ourselves—but some of us make a habit out of it. In this way we hold ourselves back from getting what we want out of life.

Dr. Amen goes on to describe the types of thinking patterns and behaviors self-sabotaging people use to get in the way of their success. It's interesting to note that none of these thoughts or actions originate in the conditions surrounding us. Self-sabotage starts *inside*. The actual circumstances of one's life have very little to do with it. Self-sabotaging people will use their particular circumstances to orchestrate their failure—no matter what those circumstances may be.

I've known people—and I'll bet you have too—who use their lack of money as the reason for their failure. I've also known people who are wealthy and use *that* as their excuse for failing. Wherever you find underachievers who blame their lack of education for their troubles, you seem to find underachievers of another kind who claim they're *over*educated, and their *excess* of schooling keeps getting in their way.

But you and I know the only thing standing in someone's way is that person alone.

What, then, *are* the things we do to sabotage our success? Though you could probably think up your own list with dozens of items on it, I've boiled it down to four items that I feel contribute most to our failure.

1. Blaming others. Dr. Amen calls this one of the most self-defeating symptoms he sees in his practice. He also says it's the first step in a dangerous slide downhill.

The practice of blaming others is particularly insidious because it looks like a good excuse; it looks like a way out. "How can you expect me to succeed when he (she, my father, my mother, my boss, take your pick) was standing in my way?"

See how easy that was? The reason this is so dangerous, as Dr. Amen points out, is that when you do it, you give those other people control over your life. You see yourself as a victim. You see yourself as the *effect* of what goes on in your life, not the cause. And you will never succeed when you are an effect, only when you are a cause.

2. Setting impossible tasks. This is also insidious, because it *looks* like you're really trying to get something done. Example: Someone who's been a bank teller for ten years decides she's in a rut and needs to break out of it in order to succeed. So she resolves to quit smoking, lose weight, start exercising, update her wardrobe, and get an MBA.

Now, none of these is an impossible task. But any one of them, by itself, is a big challenge. Trying to do them all at once is not only unrealistic, it virtually guarantees failure. If you were to hear this person telling of her plans, you'd probably wonder, does she really want to accomplish all these things—or, deep down, does she want to fail and stay where she is?

3. Setting an impossible schedule for getting tasks done. No matter how well-meaning you are, no matter how enthusiastic and intent on success, you cannot escape one basic truth about life: *things take time.* Maybe it's a symptom of our technological age: we've become so accustomed to instant gratification, we expect to find it in areas of our lives where nothing is instant.

It's like the joke about an idealistic young man who climbs to the top of a mountain to see a guru, and when he gets there he says, "I want spiritual enlightenment, and I want it *now*. I've only got two weeks' vacation."

Ridiculous as that may seem, otherwise levelheaded people make demands upon themselves that are almost as unrealistic. I remember with some sadness the case of my own father, who at 250 pounds was 100 pounds overweight. When he got into his fifties, doctors cautioned him that his excess weight could kill him in a few years. Alarmed, he went on diets, but he always tried to lose 20 pounds a week, figuring that in a month or so his weight problem would be solved. He didn't consider that it took him most of fifty years to get as heavy as he was, that his eating habits took just as many years to form, and that permanent weight loss of such magnitude might take several years to accomplish. It's also interesting that his doctors never pointed out these things either. So much for "expert" advice.

After failing at one diet after another, Dad finally gave up and just stayed heavy. He did not live to age sixty.

4. Not doing the very things we *know* we must do. This is the area where you find yourself saying, "C'mon, who're you trying to kid?" Example: you have a friend who laments his current physical condition and swears he's going to "get back in shape." So he vows to get up every morning at five o'clock and jog three miles before breakfast. Before he even starts, you know this resolution is headed for failure. He's already engaging in self-sabotaging behaviors #2 and #3—setting an impossible task and an impossible schedule. But the capper comes when you see him at work one morning and you ask, "How's the jogging?"

"Well," he replies with guilt in his voice, "there was this really great Clark Gable movie on last night, and you know my weakness for Gable. So I didn't get to sleep till after midnight, and . . ."

You know the rest. Before the sentence is out, you want to say, "C'mon, who're you trying to kid? Someone who's serious about getting fit by jogging before breakfast doesn't stay up past midnight impersonating a potato. You're not doing the very things you *know* you have to do."

If you're like most people, the hard thing to accept is that you too engage in this kind of negative, self-sabotaging behavior. You know what you have to do, but for whatever reason, you just don't do it.

—You know you should save your money, but instead of setting up an automatic savings deduction from your paycheck or your checking account, you trust your own "discipline." The discipline lasts as long as the next sale at the mall.

—You know you should start your day making sales calls when you're fresh, but instead you go to a coffee shop for an hour to "plan your day."

—You know you should get rid of the half gallon of ice cream in your freezer in order to stay with your diet, but you leave it there, "in case someone else wants some." Guess who winds up eating it?

In all of these situations, would you be surprised to hear someone say, "C'mon, who're you trying to kid?"

Starting on the Road to Success

No matter what you're trying to accomplish, no matter where you're heading, you must always start from the same place. You really have no choice: you have to start from where you are right now.

If you want a college education, it would be nice if you had a high school diploma to start with. But if you dropped out of school in the eighth grade, you don't have a high school diploma and that's the way it is. If you want to weigh 180 pounds, it would be great if you only had to take off 20. But if you now weigh 350, that's where you start from. If you want to become a millionaire, a $900,000 nest egg would be a big help. But if you now owe more than you have and you're starting from less than zero, there's no denying it.

The first step on the road to success is to acknowledge what your world really looks like, and to accept the responsibility for making it look that way.

OK, so you're broke. No use pretending you're not. No use blaming someone else for it either. Because as long as you're making someone else responsible for your financial situation, you're giving up your own power to do something about it.

OK, so you're unhappily married. But you got married of your own free will. Do you live in a country where you're forced to marry someone you don't want to? Is there anything preventing you from getting counseling, becoming separated, or getting divorced?

"We would do something about our marriage," you say, "but we don't have the money." I say, baloney. Look around: clergy people do marriage counseling for free. Most local governments provide some sort of family guidance or free legal clinics for people who want to fix up or end their marriages.

Face it: your life looks the way it does right now because you, and only you, have made it look that way. Don't heap a lot of judgment on it. Don't beat yourself up. For better or worse, just accept it. Because until you do, you won't be able to make it look like anything else.

Accepting responsibility for the way things are in your life is not easy. But once you've done it, not only are you on your way to changing it, but you're also ready for the next step. And the next step is to admit that you've been lying to yourself.

That's right, lying. If there's a condition in your life you've been meaning to change and haven't, that means you've lied to yourself about it. In all likelihood you've lied about it hundreds of times.

How many times have you said, "Boy, I've really got to quit smoking. Starting tomorrow, no more cigarettes." That's a lie, and you know it. You knew it when you said it.

How many times have you said, "I really should spend more time with the kids. Starting this Saturday, it's kids' day all day." Another lie. You *and* your kids know it.

How often have you resolved to get back to exercising, to read more and watch less TV, to spend more time working and less time goofing off, to clean out the garage, to lose weight, to cut down your drinking, to listen more to your spouse?

How many times have you lied to yourself about nearly every aspect of your life you're unsatisfied with? Certainly hundreds. More likely, thousands. Be honest with yourself right now and you'll have to admit the ratio of promises broken to promises kept is heavily on the side of the broken. Because if it weren't, then the situation wouldn't be as it is. You wouldn't *be* unsatisfied with that aspect of your life. You would have changed it long ago. And you know it.

When you lie to yourself this way, over and over, day after day, year after year, you develop a strong habit of not doing what you say you're going to do. This habit becomes so ingrained, so much a part of you, you don't even see it. People who are chronically overweight have lied to themselves so much over the years, they'll righteously claim to be on a strict diet even as they're eating a piece of cheesecake—with whipping cream on it. They've lied about this particular thing so often, they no longer hear themselves lying.

Examine any condition in your life that's persisted over time, and sooner or later you'll have to admit you've been lying to yourself about it so much, the lies have become second nature to you.

Each person has a relationship with his or her own self. For instance, you have opinions about yourself, just as you have opinions about others. You dress your body in certain ways, take care of your health in certain ways, talk to yourself in certain ways, and generally carry on all the aspects of a relationship with yourself as you would with anyone else.

By lying to yourself repeatedly over a long period of time, you've developed a relationship with yourself that lacks integrity. If you were married to yourself, you'd be demanding a divorce on the grounds of infidelity. If you were business partners with yourself, you'd be threatening to sue.

It's ironic—and even a little sad—how readily we put up with a lack of integrity in our relationships with ourselves that we would not tolerate from somebody else. If you made a date to go jogging every morning with a neighbor, and the neighbor showed up only once or twice a week, you wouldn't put up with it for ten years, would you?

At the same time, we demonstrate much less integrity with ourselves than we ever would with someone else. Turning the above situation around, you wouldn't promise your neighbor you'd meet her every morning, then not show up most of the time, would you? Even if you did, after a few weeks, you'd say you were sorry, but you just can't seem to wake up that early. The lack of integrity in the relationship would just be unbearable to you.

Yet you're more than willing to put up with much less integrity in your own relationship with yourself. And you're not alone. Look around, and you'll see a town full of people who are doing the same thing.

This, then, is how you keep yourself from succeeding:

—by refusing to accept responsibility for the way things are;
—by setting up impossible tasks for yourself;
—by setting up impossible schedules; and
—by not doing what you know you must.

In perpetrating this sabotage, you lie to yourself again and again over long periods of time, thereby developing a relationship with yourself that sorely lacks integrity.

We've already seen the beginnings of what it will take to stop your self-sabotage and get you succeeding again. First you have to take responsibility for your life as it is, and then you have to admit you're a liar. Once you've done those things, you're on the road to success.

Before we continue down that road, let's take a closer look at the objective—just to be sure that when we get there, we'll be getting what we really want. Let's take a look at success, and see if we like what it holds for us.

⇒ **4**

What Is Success, Anyway?

Nothing succeeds like success.
—Alexandre Dumas

Several years ago, as a Christmas gift, my publisher sent me a book called *The Best of Success*. It contains 333 pages of ideas and aphorisms about everything even remotely connected with success. It even has fifty-six different definitions of success, offered by everyone from Will Shakespeare to Zig Ziglar. The definitions are so wise and poignant, I was tempted to quote every one. Instead, I tried to find the best one, but I couldn't make up my mind.

I suspect there are as many definitions of success as there are people who have tried to define it, so to search for one "best" meaning is probably a waste of time. Yet I think it can be a valuable use of our time to look at a few key definitions of a word that's probably as overused and misunderstood as any in our language.

My fattest dictionary gives "success" only five definitions. The first one is "the favorable or prosperous termination of attempts or endeavors." Not as poetic as Shakespeare, but it does contain one word that I believe is the key to understanding what success is all about. That word is "termination."

An attempt or endeavor cannot be a success until it's over. In the classic baseball analogy, no one can say a game is won until the last out is made. In your case, an attempt or endeavor is not over until you say it is. This puts the control of your success, the very definition of your success, into your hands. Once you accept that, you don't ever have to accept anyone else's definition. You can succeed, or you can die trying. In either case, by your own definition, you haven't failed.

Martha Friedman says that success must be based on internal fulfillment. Any other kind will eventually ring hollow. If the fulfillment is internal, the very definition must be too.

Even though yours is the only definition of success that counts, it can help you to hear what others have to say. First, let's explore successful people's views of success. It's like learning at the knee of the master.

George Gallup, Jr., and Alec M. Gallup (as in Gallup Poll) conducted over a thousand hours of interviews with some of the most important and successful people in the United States, as reported by *Who's Who in America*. The Gallups then published their findings in their own book, *The Great American Success Story.*

After all their interviews, the Gallups were able to put together some revealing definitions of success. But the one that seems to encapsulate them all comes from John Templeton, legendary investment manager and founder of the Templeton Funds: "Success, then, can be measured by the degree to which he helps and enriches others, even as he is helping himself."

From this we can infer that those who are truly successful are those who can define their success in terms of helping other people and enriching their lives. Other definitions of success involve making the best of whatever we have to work with. Examples, taken from a variety of sources:

—"It's what you do with what you've got."
—Leroy Van Dyke
—"It is the distance between one's origins and one's final achievement."
—Michael Korda
—"Do what you can, with what you have, where you are."
—Theodore Roosevelt
—"Let each become all that he was created capable of being."
—Thomas Carlyle

—"Become all that you are capable of becoming!"

—*Robert J. McKain*

—"Be all that you can be."

—*N.W. Ayer, Inc.* (advertising campaign for the U.S. Army)

Because success can so readily be defined in your own terms, it's easy to fall into a trap. The trap is to expand the definition so far that just about anything you do is a success. When you expand the definition far enough, you eventually get to the point where the word has no value.

Here's what I mean. You decide to go back to school at night. When you start out, you define your success as earning a certain degree, say a bachelor's in business. But when you take on the task, you find out it's tougher than you thought. So you say to yourself, "I don't have to actually finish in order to be a success. Just taking the classes will help me in my job. As long as I'm enrolled and matriculating, I'm succeeding."

After a while, even this becomes too much for you. So you change your definition again. "I don't actually have to be enrolled all the time. I can enroll every second or third semester. As long as I'm intending to stay with it, that's progress, and progress is success."

See? Before long, just thinking about going back to school will fit your definition, even though for all practical purposes you've stopped trying—even though, by the dictionary's standard, your endeavor has terminated unfavorably, and you have not succeeded at all.

A Definition You Can't Weasel Out Of

Let's try to define success in a way that's flexible, but will hold you to a measurable standard over the long haul.

The definition is this: to succeed, you must constantly move to higher levels of achievement. To call yourself a success, you must be able to look at what you've done with a particular task, at a certain level, be satisfied with it, and be done with it. This is necessary, because you cannot move to the next level until you've completed what's on this one.

By this definition, the essence of success is *completion*. It's finishing what you start. In some circumstances, it may mean finishing only a part of what you start and postponing the rest, but your success can include only what you've completed—by definition.

If completion is the essence of success, then the essence of completion is integrity. And integrity is doing what you say you'll do. Integrity is action. Your words can lie, but your actions can't. It will do you no good to say, "I've completed this," when your actions plainly show you have not. Maybe that's why wise old Andrew Carnegie, the world's first billionaire, said he paid less attention to what people said, and instead just watched what they did.

Let's see how this definition of success holds up to a real-world example. Suppose you want to own and operate a successful health food store. As you go along, you find there are hundreds of actions you must perform in order to succeed at this endeavor. Get a license, rent space, build shelves, buy stock, advertise, serve customers, control inventory—you soon learn just how much action is required of you.

Throughout this venture, you can define and measure your success by what you complete. If you get a license, but then never make up your mind what space to rent, your success stops the moment you get the license, because that's the last thing you completed. The essence of success is completion.

Now suppose it's five years later, and you're merrily running your health food store. Are you a success yet? Well, this is where you have to rely on your own definition. You have to ask yourself, "What did I set out to accomplish?" If all you were trying to do is own and operate a business you enjoy, regardless of whether it was profitable or not, then you know you're a success. Some people may say you're not really a success in a business unless you're making a profit, but for you, that may not be so. For you, *at this level of achievement,* it could be that simply running the business on a break-even or slightly unprofitable basis is enough.

On the other hand, if your own definition of success included making a profit in your health food store, then if you quit before you become profitable, you have *not* succeeded—and you know it. You may be forced to close the store, build up your capital, and start again later, but that's OK. Until you do, your venture is not a success—by your own definition.

I use this example because this morning I noticed that the health food store in my neighborhood is closed and the shelves are empty. My first thought was, what a shame, the owner failed. But I quickly realized how wrong that thought could be.

Maybe the woman who ran the store had only ever wanted to see if she could do it—see if she could handle all the complexity and challenge of retail business. And maybe once she discovered she had the ability, for her the venture was completed. Once completed, it was a success— and now she is too.

Just to make it interesting, let's say her objective was completely different. Suppose what she really intended was to build up a tremendously profitable business, then sell it for a huge gain, buy a yacht, and sail off to the South Seas. If that's what she really wanted, but didn't achieve, then her actions did not match her words. She has not succeeded at the level that she chose. Therefore, for her, the venture is not complete.

At a lower level, she still has much success to be proud of. She actually ran the store for several years, feeding herself and her family all the while. She learned a great many things about business, things she can put to use the next time she tries. She acquired valuable contacts and she made mistakes she'll never make again. But on the level at which she chose to define her success, she's not done. If she quits now, she has failed at that level. And she knows it, because her own words originally defined what success would be for her. She must have the integrity to admit she did not achieve what she said she would, and therefore is not yet done.

The essence of success is completion, and the essence of completion is integrity. It's a definition you can't weasel out of.

Now that we know what success is, the next question has to be, do you really want it? This is not an easy one to answer, but after you read the next chapter, you just might be able to.

⇒ **5**

*Being a Success
While Looking
Like a Failure*

Achievement is not always success, while reputed failure often is.

—Orison Swett Marden

Some years ago, I wrote a book called *The Ultimate Secret to Getting Absolutely Everything You Want,* which discusses a principle that can lead people to success. The principle is this: in order to accomplish something, you must be willing to do whatever it takes to accomplish it. The principle holds that in order to get what you want, you don't *necessarily* have to do anything. The very power of your willingness—the force of your commitment—may cause you to get results with little or no effort. The principle also recognizes that, even when your commitment is absolute, you almost always have to do *some*thing—but you never know in advance how much that something will be.

Since *The Ultimate Secret* was released, I've

been interviewed over a hundred times—on radio and television, and for newspapers and magazines. I particularly enjoy appearing on radio shows where the audience is allowed to call in and ask questions. At those times, I get to deal with real people, their hopes and dreams, successes and failures.

When I first started doing the interviews, I was amazed at how many people said they had a burning desire to accomplish a particular goal, yet admitted they had never done anything to help themselves actually accomplish it. I've heard the story so many times, I'm no longer surprised by it.

A man in Springfield, Massachusetts, says he wants a better job, yet admits that in five years, he has not even looked for one. A young woman in San Jose says she wants to make a lot of money in real estate, yet concedes she's never taken the time to learn how—even though people she knows have gotten wealthy literally in her own backyard.

Some folks say they need help, yet never ask for it. I talked to a woman in Phoenix who was disabled, and badly in need of a wheelchair, but couldn't afford one. On the radio, she admitted she had never made a phone call or asked anyone for advice or assistance. She was astounded when I mentioned that volunteer organizations often donate wheelchairs to people who need them. Then she was overjoyed when an official of one of those organizations heard the conversation on the air and within minutes called and offered one to her.

My point is, while most people genuinely want to succeed, and recognize that they must be willing to do everything it takes, those same people are often unwilling to do even the *first* thing. After all those interviews, I think I've finally figured out why they don't take action. The reason is, most people have been given a faulty definition of failure, and this definition, this mistaken notion, is holding them back. It's quite possible this same mistaken notion is holding you back too.

The Real Difference Between Success and Failure

If you were asked to define failure, it wouldn't be surprising if you responded as most people do. You might say something like "It's when you try for something and you don't get it. Successful people are those who make it; failures are those who don't."

This kind of response would be evidence that you'd been given a mistaken notion of what failure is all about. Failure is not about trying and not achieving. Failure is about *not trying,* or *giving up* after trying too little.

The difference between a success and a failure is not that the success tried and succeeded while the failure tried and didn't succeed. A success is a person who *tries and tries.* A failure is a person who *tries and quits,* or doesn't try at all.

A person who tries something has the *possibility* of not achieving it. A person who doesn't try has the *certainty* of not achieving it.

In early 1990, I was being interviewed on a radio talk show in Texas. We were discussing my second book, *The Secret to Conquering Fear.* The caller was a woman who wanted to take a new job in a new career, and even though she was unemployed at the time, she was afraid to make the move.

After we discussed the reasons for her fear, and the emotions underlying them, I asked, "If you took the job, what are the chances you could call this station on this date in 1991 and report that you had succeeded in your new career?"

"About 50–50, maybe better," she allowed.

"Now, if you *don't* take the job, what are the chances you could call a year from now and say you'd succeeded?"

Silence.

In that moment, the woman realized that by

giving in to the fear and not trying, she was *guaranteeing* she would wind up with what she feared most—not succeeding in the new job.

What about you? How many times in your life, because of a misplaced fear of failure, have you avoided trying something?

What about the time back in school when you wanted to try out for the team, but you didn't because you dreaded the embarrassment of not making it?

What about the job opportunity you turned down—because it was in another town, and if it didn't work out, you'd be alone and broke in a strange place?

What about all the hundreds of things you've wanted to try, but didn't because you were uncertain about the outcome: investments, journeys, relationships, contests, competitions, adventures? It doesn't take a statistician to figure out that you failed at 100 percent of the ones you didn't try.

In a nutshell, the message is this: the only true success is the person who's trying; the only true failure is the one who isn't.

When you avoid trying because of a fear of failure, you are living a lie. Because the truth is, every time you try, you accomplish *something*. Every time you try, you learn—even if it's only what not to do on your next try. We've all heard some variation of the story about the

time an interviewer asked Thomas Edison why
he kept trying to find a material for the fila-
ment in his light bulb, even though he had
failed in over a thousand attempts. He replied
that he wasn't discouraged because all those attempts had given him over a thousand materi-
als that he was sure would *not* work. Edison
saw those thousand attempts, not as failures,
but as a thousand steps to success.

Remember when you were a toddler, teaching
yourself to walk, and you fell down a thousand
times? Did you think of those thousand bumps
on the rump as failures—or did you, like
Thomas Edison, see them as steps to success?

Now, what if Thomas Edison had died before
he discovered the material that worked? Would
we consider him a failure? Maybe not. Someone
else could have picked up where he left off and
found it anyway, and history may have recog-
nized Edison for the valuable groundwork he
laid for the eventual discovery.

What I'm trying to say is, if Edison had loved
what he was doing and had died trying, he
might have been as much a success as anyone
who ever reached a goal before death.

I know a woman in Los Angeles who wants to
be an actress more than anything else in the
world. If you know anything about L.A., you
know the town is full of people who want exactly what she does. Most of them make their

living parking cars or waiting tables, while in their spare time they show up at one casting call after another, hoping to land the key role that will launch their careers. For over five years now, Jenny has been one of those people.

I'm no Hollywood talent scout, but I have seen Jenny act, and in my opinion, she's terrible. In real life, she has a marvelous, bubbling personality, coupled with genuineness and honesty that simply charm anyone she meets. When she acts, none of that comes through. How she ever gets roles, I don't know. But she gets them. I suppose, by the sheer effort of auditioning for anything she can.

If you were to ask Jenny what she does for a living, she would instantly reply, "I'm an actress," even though she spends no more than two weeks out of any year acting, and probably gets less than 5 percent of her income from it.

For her, any hint of interest from an agent is a cause for great joy. Any small role she lands is a great victory. To spend two days waiting around, then to appear for five seconds on the screen as an extra—for her, that's a major success.

One day, Jenny may make it big in Hollywood, and I hope she does, because no one in that town will have earned it more. But even if she doesn't, until or unless she gives up, she's not a failure, and no one can make her a failure just by saying she is. She may become a star, or she may die trying. Either way, she gives us something to admire. Either way, she teaches us something about success and failure.

To die while attempting to get what you want is not failure. To die without attempting—*that* is failure.

Following Your Inner Agenda

OK, so now we know the real difference between success and failure. The question still remains: do you want success or not? Answering this question may take some independent thought on your part, and it may take some courage. Here's why.

Most contemporary notions of success are based on measurable, physical evidence, and this evidence is often widely accepted. Let me tell you about Rebecca, a young woman I know in San Diego. She's thirty-one years old, good-looking, and well-educated. She works at a used book store in town and annually ranks near the top of the sales force in commissions. Rebecca's wardrobe is the envy of every woman who meets her. Her car payment is larger than most people's salaries, and she just bought a condominium with a breathtaking view of San Diego Bay. It would not be unreasonable to say

Rebecca's life fits most people's notion of success. That's because we can count the money and see the car and calculate the value of the condo.

Now let me tell you about a man I know, also in San Diego, who works as a gardener and barely makes enough money to feed his wife and five children. Joe has no money saved, owns nothing besides his gardening tools, and is always a day or two away from being evicted from his apartment. Most people would agree Joe is not a success.

But let me round out these two pictures a bit. Rebecca lives in almost constant anxiety, because she can't seem to make a relationship work. She's gone out with dozens of men and become seriously involved with several. But none of them will commit to a long-term relationship with her. Her friendships don't fare much better. She has many casual acquaintances, but no real friends. On weekends, she often spends all her time alone because she has no one to call, no one who's happy to hear her voice. Rebecca works late almost every night. Though her condo is beautiful, she hates to go home to the emptiness of it.

By contrast, Joe loves to go home every night because when he does, his children jump all over him and scream with delight. His wife lovingly prepares his favorite food, and every so of-

ten saves up enough spare change to treat him
and the children to a dish of ice cream to go with
it. Would you still say Joe is less successful
than Rebecca?

Success—true success—does not always
come in forms that are visible or measurable.
You can't see or measure how someone feels as
they make their way home at the end of a work-
day. Yet *they* know. For successful people to get
where they are, they had to think independently enough to say, "*This* is what I want in
life. It may not be what other people want, but
it's what I want, and to me, this is what counts."

Such people also have to have the courage to
pursue and preserve their own notions of success, despite the criticism and discouragement
others may heap upon them.

What about the man who gives up all his possessions, leaves his family and friends, becomes
a Trappist monk, and lives a life of prayer, hard
work, and silence until he dies? Is he a success?

What about the doctor who turns down a potentially lucrative practice to do the research
she loves—even though her laboratory is badly
underfunded and her work goes unappreci-
ated? Is she a success?

What about the government employee who
blows the whistle on widespread graft and cor-
ruption, but loses his job and his pension as a
result? Is he a success?

What about you? Are you able to think independently enough to form your own vision of success, even though it looks like failure to everyone else? Do you have the courage to endure the pressures and criticisms of those close to you who refuse to accept your vision?

These are questions only you can answer. The good news is, yours is the only answer that means anything. Only you can say what success is—for you. Only you can define your failure.

Carol Burnett, whose career on stage, television, and in films could be considered successful by anyone's standards, uses her own standard to grade herself. When asked about her many flops, she replied, "If I like my own performance I'm not nearly as bothered as I am when I don't like what I've done. That's when I want to kick myself—when something I've done flops and I don't like my work. If I like what I've done—even if no one else likes it—I can handle the failure much easier."

As with Ms. Burnett, your own definitions of success and failure must be internal and personal.

It doesn't stop there. Just as only you can say what success or failure is, only you can determine what your rewards will be for success—and what punishments you'll endure for failure. This is very important, because if you want to succeed, you'd be wise to encourage behavior that leads to success and discourage behavior that leads to failure.

If you're an adult, and if you know what you want, you're responsible for your own success. It's up to you to define it, to achieve it, and to know it when you've got it. It's also your responsibility to discard what you've achieved when you realize it's not what you thought it would be.

So, now that you know what success is, now that you know the independence, the courage, and the responsibility success will demand of you, do you still want to succeed?

I thought so.

To do it, here's all you need.

⇒ **6**

All You Need In Order to Succeed

All great changes are irksome to the human mind, especially those which are attended with great dangers and uncertain effects.

—John Adams

The fact that you're halfway through this book and still reading should tell you something about yourself. Chances are, you'd like to succeed at some endeavor, but as yet you haven't. If this is the case, logic says you must make some kind of change in your life.

It stands to reason: what you've done so far has gotten you what and where you are now. If you want to have something different, if you want to be somewhere different, then you have to *do* something different. Logical and obvious as this may sound, you'd be amazed at how many people keep doing the same things over and over, year after year, hoping to get a different result. That doesn't work. What works is *change*.

The first thing you have to change is your mind. This is also the hardest thing. If you've ever tried to get someone else to change his or her mind, you know why: the human mind resists change. It often cannot see its own errors, though they may be blatantly obvious to anyone else. And just when the mind appears to have changed, it slips back into thinking as it did before.

Changing the mind can be frustrating, maddening, doubly difficult because there's nothing physically visible or measurable to it. But it's necessary, because you can't change your actions until you change your mind.

In their book, *I Can If I Want To,* Arnold Lazarus, Ph.D., and Allen Fay, M.D., say four conditions are necessary for any kind of change to occur:

1. You must *identify* something as a problem.
2. You must *accept the possibility* that something can be done about it.
3. You must *express a desire* to change.
4. You must *be willing to work* and make an effort to change.

These four conditions apply readily to the task of changing your mind. Example: for years you've been working for someone else, but you really want to be in business for yourself. What's been holding you back is, all along you've honestly believed you can't make it on your own. If you're going to open that business, what you have to do first is change your mind.

Can you identify a problem? "Well," you say, "I don't exactly dislike my work, and the pay is good enough, and the benefits are better than I could afford if I were on my own. Plus, I have job security and a pension when I retire."

If that's all you have to say, you might as well forget about going into business for yourself. On the other hand, if after all that, you still say, *"But . . ."*—then you may have a problem.

"But I still want to see if I can make it on my own. . . . But I hate taking orders from a guy who knows less than I do. . . . But unless I'm challenged, I'll go crazy with boredom. . . . But . . . but . . . but." Every one of these "buts" signals a possible trouble spot. If you can positively say, "I really won't be satisfied until I get rid of that 'but,' " then you've identified a problem.

And you've just taken the first step toward changing your mind.

Now, will you accept the possibility that something can be done about it? "I've never gone into business before," you may say. "I wouldn't know where to begin. I don't have any start-up capital saved. I don't even know what kind of business I want to try."

Fine, but will you admit it's possible for you to *ask* someone where to begin? Will you admit it's possible for you to start, right now, to save money? Can you accept that you have the ability to explore various business opportunities to see what appeals to you?

If you answered yes to any of those questions, you've taken the second step to changing your mind.

Got the idea? By the time you've completed Step 4, it's entirely possible that for the first time in your life, you will have changed your mind about going into business for yourself. That alone is a tremendous accomplishment. But it's just the beginning. Next, you must change your *behavior*. That's not easy either, and so we'll spend almost all of the rest of this book talking about it. But before we do, let's quickly look at what you *don't* need and what you *do* need in order to succeed.

No matter what anybody tells you, you *don't* need money, or an education, or an established position, or connections, or a lot of brains, or even good health. In every country on earth, in every period of history, there have been people who succeeded mightily without any of those things. If you think the lack of one of these items has been keeping you from succeeding, *change your mind*. You don't need it.

What then *do* you need?

To find out, you could ask those who have already succeeded, as the Gallups did in *The Great American Success Story*. When asked to name the characteristics of successful people, the respondents gave these answers, in order of frequency:

1. Common sense
2. Special knowledge
3. Self-reliance
4. General intelligence
5. Ability to get things done
6. Leadership
7. Knowing right from wrong
8. Creativity and inventiveness
9. Self-confidence
10. Oral expression
11. Concern for others
12. Luck

Take a few moments to contemplate these, and you'll see the majority of them, like common sense, general intelligence, and self-confidence, are characteristics you were born with. In other words, some of the most successful people in the world are saying you started out in life with most of what you needed in order to succeed.

But even if you've lost these characteristics, even if you've *forgotten* how to use them, can you still succeed?

To find out, let's go all the way back to the beginning, when you first started out. When you were that tiny organism, you were driven by a powerful, instinctive desire to survive and grow. The desire was so strong, you were willing to risk everything—even your life—in order to make it a reality.

The first time you succeeded, all you had was desire and commitment. As it turned out, that was all you needed. And guess what: that's all you need today. If you have a strong desire to accomplish something, and the willingness to do whatever it takes to get it, you can succeed. Desire and commitment; those are the only real necessities. Everything else is optional.

You might find it interesting that these two elements just happen to be an intensified version of the last two of Drs. Lazarus and Fay's four conditions for change: *express a desire*, and *be willing to work*.

Let's say that as of this moment, you already have those things to the appropriate degree. You already have the burning desire; you're already willing to do whatever it takes. Now you want to know *how* to do it. You want to know what you have to do in order to succeed.

For this, it will help you a great deal to recall The Forgotten Secret. And at long last, here it is.

$\Rightarrow$ **7**

The
Forgotten
Secret

Just do it.
—Advertising slogan for Nike
athletic wear

In the very beginning, when your success mechanism was working unimpeded, you were using a secret principle, a principle you knew instinctively. It was a simple principle, and when you chose to apply it, it worked every time. The way you activated this principle was simple too. You set your sights on a particular objective, then proceeded to do what you had to do in order to reach it.

When you used this principle effectively, there was unity between what you made up your mind to do and what you actually tried to do. When you put the principle to work, your *word* and your *deed* were the same.

If you tried and didn't accomplish what you wanted, you automatically tried again, as soon as you could. And you kept trying, until your objective was no longer desirable. You kept going for it and going for it and going for it—until you got it, or until you no longer wanted it. You didn't know the meaning of such words as "failure," "discouragement," "self-doubt," "impossible," "unrealistic," or "unreasonable."

"Sure, sure," you say, "everybody knows this. 'If at first you don't succeed, try, try, try again.' What's the big secret?"

The big secret—the Forgotten Secret—is this:

In order to succeed at anything, keep your word.

Do the thing you say you will do and your success is inevitable. Keep your word. Do what you say. And you'll succeed.

Among successful people, this principle is so obvious, so thoroughly embedded in their unconscious, they don't even mention it when they're asked what it takes to succeed. They say success calls for characteristics like "common sense," "special knowledge," and "self-reliance." But those responses are on an intellectual level. On the practical level, super-achievers simply make up their minds to go after something, then just go after it.

In the words of Judi Missett, the founder of

Jazzercise, "Dream your biggest, most terrific dreams. Then, work your ass off."

Unsuccessful people *talk* about what they're going to do. They make elaborate plans. They set up schedules and agendas. They take classes and ask advice. Then, they find other things to do that seem more important. They become distracted. They lose interest. They begin to doubt, first their own desire for the objective, then their ability to achieve it.

After a while, unsuccessful people let their elaborate plans slip. They revise their schedules. When someone gives them negative advice, they take it to heart. They forget. They neglect to follow through. They procrastinate. Finally, they abandon the objective, but not until they've compiled a whole list of reasons why it wasn't a good idea in the first place.

Unsuccessful people share one trait in common: they are liars. They lie to themselves and they lie to others. All those elaborate plans and schedules are a big lie—just a way of making it *look* as if they're doing something to reach their goal. When they say they want advice on how to get something done, they're lying. What they really want is to hear why it *can't* be done, so they can have an excuse, ratified by an "expert," for not doing it.

When they say they didn't have time, the truth is they didn't *take* the time.

When they say someone got in their way, the truth is they *allowed* someone to get in their way.

When they say they couldn't find what they were looking for, the truth is, they didn't *look*—or didn't look far enough.

When they say they didn't have the money, the truth is they didn't go out and round up the money they knew it would take.

When they say they tried, the truth is they didn't try very hard, or they didn't try at all.

Do you hear yourself in any of these lies? If so, don't be surprised, and don't be ashamed. You could be lying this way for any number of reasons, some of them so deeply unconscious it would take years of therapy to get to the bottom of them.

But you may not want or need therapy. All you may need is some practice in using the Forgotten Secret. All you may need is to start making a change. All you may need is to start *acting* like a successful person.

If you want to succeed at anything, keep your word. Do that, and you'll be acting like a successful person.

Yes, successful people make plans. But they're implementing those plans even as the ink is drying. Often they get started before the plans are fully developed. They can't wait.

Yes, successful people make schedules. But if

the schedule starts getting in the way, they revise it, or abandon it, and get on with the job.

Yes, successful people ask for advice. But if the advice is negative or discouraging, they go "deaf." When some expert says they can't or shouldn't do something they really want to do, they just don't hear it. In fact, "selective deafness" is a trait possessed by an uncommonly high percentage of successful people I've met.

Yes, successful people are short of time. But they always seem to find the time to do what really needs to get done. Did you ever notice how the most successful people are always being asked to do just one more thing? And they fit it in, somehow?

Yes, successful people find others in their way. But they push them aside, or get them to help, rather than hinder.

Yes, successful people have money problems. In fact, most successful people can't afford what they set out to do. But they know the supply of money in the world is unlimited, so they find supporters, sponsors, investors, lenders, or donors.

And no, successful people don't say, "I tried." They say, "I'm trying." They say, "I'm working on it." If they tried and failed, they say, "It didn't pan out—but I learned a lot." And they're telling the truth.

Do you want to be a successful person? Just

tell the truth. Whatever you say you're going to do, just do. If you know you're probably not going to do something, don't bother to say you will. In your personal morality code, make it the most serious kind of sin to tell a lie to yourself. Allow nothing to be as sacred as your own word. Make this one change in your life, and your whole life will change. Guaranteed.

To help you make this change, I'm going to give you a key, a golden key.

⇒ **8**

*The
Golden
Key*

Giving opens the way for receiving.

—Florence Scovel Shinn

If you boil them down to their essence, all definitions of success have one thing in common. They all say that success involves formation of and movement toward a goal. It stands to reason: if you want to get anywhere, you have to know where you're going. By the same token, if you don't have a goal, how will you ever know when you've succeeded? So whether you like it or not, if you want to succeed, you'll need some sort of method for goal-setting.

There are plenty of goal-setting methods for you to choose from. The self-help section of any bookstore or library is bound to have at least one or two books advising you how to do it. I'm not going to repeat any of the methods described in those books; nor am I going to suggest a new one. From what I've seen, there is an abundance of proven techniques available for setting clear, achievable, measurable goals. Take your pick, or make one up. What's important is not *how* you set your goals; the important thing is *doing* it.

Before you begin, I'd like to remind you of a principle, one you may already know, but which it is necessary to bring to mind whenever you set a goal for yourself. The principle is this: *all true success flows out of giving something to someone.* If you want something for yourself, you have to give something to another. This is not only a pretty good moral principle, it's also the basis for successful relationships and the foundation of any profitable business.

If you really want to do a good job of stating a goal, state it in terms of what you will give, what service you will provide, what good you will do for people. Even if your goal seems to benefit no one but you, find a way to make it help others. If your goal is to quit smoking or lose weight, frame it in terms of the joy you'll give your family members by living a longer and healthier life. If you have no family, resolve to set aside the money you save by not buying cigarettes or snacks, and give it to someone in need. This will elevate you to a level of resolve you could never attain if you were doing it just for yourself. And when you do give to someone, you get the extra reward of seeing them benefit.

On the other hand, to say, "My goal is to make one million dollars before I am thirty-five years old," is an almost worthless statement. Nobody's going to give you a million dollars just for getting up in the morning from now until you turn thirty-five. But there are plenty of things people *will* give you a million dollars for. Inventing a better personal computer. Writing a best-seller. Finding a cure for the common cold.

Notice that the three things I just mentioned will give people something they want: more efficient offices, a pleasurable reading experience, better health.

Success involves getting something you want; it consists of having something desirable flow to you. But *giving,* not taking, always starts this flow. That's why you always have to state your goals in terms of what you will give. When all you're interested in is taking, people will try to stop you from succeeding. By contrast, when they see you're interested in giving, people will try to help you succeed—*even though in both cases the goal may be exactly the same.*

"That'd be great if I knew what my goals are," you may say, "but I don't even know what I want." This is a common lament. As someone who writes and speaks about achievement, I hear it wherever I go. If that's your problem, try this advice.

First, ask yourself what you really, really love to do. And don't say, "Nothing"—because everybody loves to do *some*thing. Look at how you spend your free time. Look at what you do when all your regular responsibilities are taken care of. These are the things you love to do.

Next, ask yourself how you can do that—and in the process, give something valuable to someone. There is practically no activity on earth you can't adapt in some way for the benefit of others. Let's take an extreme example.

Suppose all you really like to do is watch television. You're happiest when you're a semivegetable, staring at whatever the stations happen to be serving up for your enjoyment at any given moment. Can you possibly help your fellow man by watching television?

Well, if you happen to have a way with words, you could become a TV critic, and write evaluations of TV shows for your local newspaper. Or, if you have a sharp eye, you could offer to give your local stations your "typical viewer's" opinion of their programming—for a fee, of course.

Name just about any legal activity, and after applying some thought to it, you can find at least a few ways to benefit others by engaging in it. Remember: if you can find a way to benefit others, they'll find a way to encourage you—by giving you what you want. And that's the golden key to success.

But let's not lose touch with our principle: *success comes to those who keep their word.* Even if you have well-defined goals, the accomplishment of which will benefit people mightily, if you don't actually *do* what you say, you still won't succeed. In forming your goals, you may make promises to yourself that you have every intention of keeping. Yet if you consistently neglect to turn those intentions into actions, you're bound to fail.

If that's the way you are, you need a method that will help you keep your word. Here's one you can use every day of your life.

⇒ **9**

A Simple Method
For Making
the Secret Work

*We first make our habits, and
then our habits make us.*
                    —John Dryden

In the hundred years or so that psychology has existed as a formal field of study, it has given us a great deal. But among the greatest gifts we've ever received from the study of psychology is one of its most basic concepts—something college and even high school students learn in their introductory psych courses. Once we understand the concept, we can use it to help ourselves accomplish phenomenal feats.

The concept is this: *behavior that is rewarded is repeated.* How do you train an animal? You encourage the animal to perform a certain behavior, and when it does what you want—or something close—you give it a treat. How do you teach a child? You show or tell the child what you want, and when the child responds in the way you want, you say, "Very good," in a warm, approving voice and you pat the child on the head. How do you get beginning salespeople to boost their sales? You give them a quota— and when they exceed it, you give them a bonus.

That's reward. That's positive reinforcement. It's basic psychology. And it's so powerful, some business writers have called it the greatest management principle in the world.

You can use this principle, starting right now, to create all the success you want. You do it simply by setting up a system of rewards for yourself.

Earlier we learned that to make a change in your life, first you have to change your mind and then you have to change your behavior. Let's assume you've already changed your mind. You've convinced yourself the goal you want to achieve is desirable and achievable, and now you're ready to go for it. Now you're ready to start.

The Most Important Step

No matter what you do, you have to start with a first step. But it's very important to choose your first step carefully, because you want it to lead to the next step and the next. If you don't get past the first step, you're right where you started and you've reinforced what may be an old pattern of failure. So be very particular about that first step.

Suppose, for example, you're a salesperson and your goal is to double your sales volume within a year. When salespeople think about those kinds of goals, they immediately see themselves working longer hours, making more "cold" calls, enduring more rejection—all of which are negative, unrewarding experiences. If you decide the first step toward your goal will be to make more cold calls, you won't want to do it. You may seriously resolve to do it, but you'll break your word, just as you have so many times in the past. Even if your initial resolve carries you to the point of actually making those calls, the very act of making them will be a form of punishment. Psychology tells us to reward, not punish, the behavior we want to repeat.

"Well," you think, "I'll just reward myself *after* I've made the calls. When I've done a certain number of them, I'll treat myself to a nice dinner." Not a bad idea, and a fairly common one. But I don't think it's good enough, simply because many people tend to treat themselves to the dinner whether they make the calls or not.

I believe that if you want to get off to a good,

solid start, you need to make your first step *doubly* rewarding. That means you want to start with an action both enjoyable in the doing and rewarding when it's done.

Going back to our example, let's say the part of your job you most enjoy is figuring out new applications for the product you sell, and showing those applications to your clients. I say make *that* your first step. Take the time to come up with some truly dazzling new applications, then work them into a new presentation to take on the road with you. This way, the very act of taking your first step is rewarding in itself. Of course, you can still reward yourself with a nice dinner when you're through. By doing that, you've positively reinforced your new actions, even if they didn't result in a sale on the first try.

Remember the guidelines for your first step: enjoyable action, rewarding result. When you start that way, you're greatly increasing the likelihood you'll repeat the desired behavior.

Sooner or later, however, you're going to have to do things that aren't inherently enjoyable. It's all right; you'll have plenty of opportunity to do such things later. For now, you're trying to establish a new pattern of behavior, a new habit of success. And the surest way to do that is with reward.

Unlimited Goals, Limited Actions

People who've failed in the past often con-
clude that the reason they failed was that they
set their sights too high. "I shouldn't have
aimed at doubling my sales in a year," they say.
"That's unrealistic. No wonder I didn't make it.
I'll just shoot for ten percent per year."

I believe this is a mistake. I don't think it's
possible to set your sights too high. Remember
the words of Judi Missett: "Dream your biggest, most terrific dreams," she said—and *did*.
Lowering your goals is not necessarily going to
increase your chances of reaching them. In
fact, it may have just the opposite effect. Your
biggest dreams captivate your imagination
and give birth to your biggest and best ideas. A
tremendous challenge is a great motivator. A
tiny, easy challenge is no challenge at all; it's a
bore.

The mistake most people make is not in the
way they define their goals. The mistake is in
the way they define the actions they'll take to
work toward those goals. If you're a hundred
pounds overweight, it's entirely proper to make
a hundred-pound weight loss your goal. But it's
ridiculous to expect you'll go from 3,500 calories
a day to 800 with nothing but will power—and
lose those hundred pounds in a month.

To increase the likelihood of your success, set up a course of action that:

1. You *know* you will follow,
2. You will enjoy doing, and
3. Has a reward attached to each task.

Let's say your goal is to get into really good physical shape. Right now, you do nothing for physical fitness. Just *watching* people jog makes you tired, and walking all the way to the refrigerator for your next beer is the most exercise you get all day. You've read that to be in the kind of shape you're hoping for, you need to engage in sustained aerobic activity for at least thirty minutes, at least three times a week. That's your goal. What's your first step?

Think of something of a physical nature you already enjoy doing. Maybe it's taking a walk in the park. Fine. You decide to start your fitness program by taking a walk in the park, followed immediately by something else you enjoy . . . let's say, a cup of really good espresso. Now decide how often you'll do it to start with. Be realistic. Remember the Forgotten Secret: keep your word. What level of activity are you willing to commit to that will enable you to keep your word? Once a week? Once every two weeks? It doesn't matter. What's important is selecting a course of action you *know* you'll follow. For right now, don't be concerned about doing too little. On the contrary, if you're keeping your word and changing your behavior, you're actually doing a lot.

Start your new pattern of activity. Take a walk in the park, cap it off with that espresso you enjoy, and just feel good about yourself. Do this as often as you said you would. Every time you do, you're reinforcing your target behavior. Every time you do, you're developing a habit. And when you form a habit, you have one of the most powerful forces on earth working for you. The combined forces of desire (what you want) plus habit (what you do) equal success.

As you go along, sooner or later you'll have to perform some tasks that aren't necessarily pleasant. For example, some days you may have to walk in the rain, or the cold, or the dark—and your espresso shop may be closed. Do the unpleasant task anyway, but attach *some* kind of reward to it. Take a nice hot bath afterward, watch a favorite program, anything that specifically rewards and reinforces the course of action that's taking you to your goal.

Once you've completed the first level of action, you're ready to go on to the next behavior. Before you do, stop and assess. Notice you've completed something. It may not be much (maybe four walks in the park over a month's time), but it is a tangible, measurable accomplishment. For one month, you unified your words and your actions. You did what you said you were going to do. You began forming an important new habit. You enjoyed yourself. You did yourself some good.

But the most important part of your accomplishment is the completion, because if you recall our definition of success, it's *completion* that counts. And according to that definition, you have succeeded. You *are* a success.

What's next? Go on to the next behavior. In practice, this is just a repeat of what you just completed, except on a different level. Follow the same principles, being careful to make your first step on the new level doubly enjoyable and being extra careful that your actions duplicate your words.

From then on, just keep doing this over and over, moving from one level to the next. Force of habit is extremely powerful, and once you've got it working for you in a positive way, success will come easily and naturally—the way it did before you forgot the Secret. Pythagoras, the ancient Greek philosopher and mathematician, said, "Choose always the way that seems best, however rough it may be, and custom will soon render it easy and agreeable."

But don't be discouraged if success comes slowly. Remember, you're trying to undo years of bad habits and overcome thousands of little lies. In fact, it's better if success doesn't come too quickly. More often than not, quick success brings anxiety with it, a feeling that your success is a fluke, you didn't really earn it, and you'll be "found out." You might also feel guilty about your success—and this might lead you right back to sabotaging it, as you did before. Take your time, keep your word, and success will come according to its own schedule.

When You Don't Keep Your Word

Habit, as we know, is one of the strongest forces in our lives. It governs everything we do, whether we know it or not. Your current habits got you where you are today. So don't be surprised if your old habits overcome the patterns of your new behavior program, and you slip back into lying, excusing, justifying, and rationalizing. This should not discourage you. It should just remind you of how powerful habits are.

If you find you're not keeping your word, if you're not doing what you said you would, stop and see if you can figure out why.

Is it because you're resolving to do an unpleasant task, and you're giving yourself an inadequate reward? If so, there are two things you can do: (1) convert the unpleasant task to a pleasant one, at least temporarily, or (2) if that's not possible, beef up the reward you give yourself for doing it.

If, on the other hand, you see that the task is pleasant enough and the reward is adequate, and you're still not doing it, then it's time to check your motivation. Here's how that works.

In order to make your behavior match your word, you have to be tremendously motivated—as you were when you first taught yourself to walk. If your motivation is high enough, it will carry you; it will impel you to do the most unpleasant tasks. If it's not high enough, you have to set up a behavior that matches the level of your motivation, as I just suggested.

When that doesn't work, when you won't do the new behavior no matter how high the reward, you may just have to admit you're not motivated enough to pursue this particular goal, and instead choose another one. In other words, if you're not willing to do the very things you yourself set up to take you to your goal, you must not want it badly enough. In that case, you're better off finding something you do want badly enough and going after that. When something in your life is clearly not working, get off it and go on to something else.

You may find, for example, that no matter how many times you resolve to stay at work later, so as to get ahead in your job, you just can't bring yourself to do it. Being at home when your children are awake may be more important to you. If so, that's fine. Go home and work on becoming a better parent, especially if that motivates you more than your job.

Whatever you do, don't keep breaking your word. Don't keep saying, "I've really got to put in some more hours at the office," yet repeatedly knocking off early. All you'll be doing is reinforcing your earlier pattern of dishonesty with yourself, strengthening your previous bad habits, and repeating your history of failure.

The goal you're abandoning may be important, but if it's not important enough to you to go after it—*right now*—then you're better off abandoning it. Maybe you can come back and try it again—after you've successfully reached some other goal. If you never reach it, don't beat yourself up. Not everybody is motivated to pursue the same goals. And that's fine. If we all wanted exactly the same things, what a boring world this would be.

If you didn't follow through on a goal you weren't sufficiently motivated to pursue, don't worry about it. What's far more important is that you *do* follow through on another one—one that gives you the experience of completion and success. Get *that* experience. Feel what it's like. If necessary, take the path of least resistance on the road to success, but make sure it's success, not failure, you're experiencing. Once you've formed and solidified the habit of keeping your word, then you can go back and take on some of the goals you postponed earlier. When you do, your track record of integrity, completion, and success can carry you. If you come back a winner, you're more likely to keep winning.

⇒ **10**

Unexpected Bonus:
The "Slingshot" Effect

Instead of rising rapidly in the beginning and flattening out later, the earnings curves of most of those who eventually became millionaires was the reverse: their incomes increased slowly . . . then . . . suddenly went through the roof.

—Srully Blotnick

It's a simple, but powerful idea: *in order to succeed at anything, keep your word.* With this idea, you have already accomplished great things, phenomenal things. With this idea, you can accomplish still more—more than most people ever dream of.

What makes this simple idea so powerful? In a word, *integrity.* And what is that? I've heard it defined as "honesty when nobody's looking," but to me it's a complete and total agreement between what you say and what you do. It comes from a word that means whole, entire, undiminished. What appears to be and what really is—are exactly the same.

The power of integrity is almost unfathomable. How would it change the world if heads of state had complete integrity? How would your life be different today if the President of the Soviet Union were to say, "As long as I'm in charge, the Soviet Union will not attack another country"—and he had absolute integrity?

How would your life be different today if the politician who promised not to raise taxes had complete integrity? If the business leader who promised to stop polluting was good on his word? If the person you married kept the vows he or she made at the altar?

How would your life be different today if you had kept the promises *you've* made—to your parents, your teachers, your bosses, your spouse(s), yourself? It's almost too mind-boggling to consider.

Of all your promises, the most important ones are those you make to yourself. Since ancient times, the wise have been advising us how important it is to be true to ourselves. If I took the time, I could probably string out a list of quotes many pages long from every great thinker of the past three thousand years giving us a variation of "To thine own self be true."

What did these great minds know? Simply this: when you keep your word to yourself, you harness a great power. When there is integrity—an entirety, a wholeness—in what you say and do, you are consciously resurrecting the incredibly powerful success mechanism you used instinctively from the time you first came to be.

When you begin to keep your word to yourself, amazing things start happening. Little stumbling blocks that have been in your way start to disappear. That nagging difficulty with starting your car—you know, the thing that keeps making you late, and that you keep saying you're going to take care of—when you keep your word, it will disappear and suddenly you won't be late anymore.

When you keep your word, you see yourself as more capable and you become more confident. That resolution you keep making—you know, the one where you say you're going to get out and exercise three times a week—if you actually went out and did it, faithfully for a whole month—or three months, or six—you'd feel so capable, so proud, so confident, you might try almost anything.

When you keep your word, you experience what I call "the slingshot effect." Here's how it happens.

For years, you've been putting off something you know you should do, but just can't seem to. You've promised yourself a thousand times, and you've even made a few halfhearted tries, but you never got very far. If you use the Forgotten Secret on your very next try, and you actually do what you say, you're almost sure to find the first few steps are just as difficult—even with our double-reward system. But after a while, a mysterious phenomenon starts to occur. After a while, some of the subsequent steps that used to trip you up suddenly become easier, or unnecessary, or are done for you. Before you know it, you're farther along than you thought. One success is building on another, and you're on your way to completion at incredible speed—as if you'd been propelled from a slingshot.

When you keep your word, people change the way they perceive you. Comments like "Yeah, old Jack, he's all talk" start to change to "Jack said he was going to do that, and look at him. He's stumbling and bumbling, but he's doing it."

When you keep your word, people begin to see you as being more trustworthy. So they begin giving you more responsibility and more important tasks. When they see you completing things on one level, they give you the opportunity to move to higher levels of challenge and achievement.

I know of not one manager in any organization—profit-making or otherwise—who isn't looking for people who can be trusted, people who can be counted on to do what they say, people who can complete what they start. If you become known as one of those people, managers will start outbidding each other to get you. They'll keep paying higher and higher prices, just to have you on their team.

Before long, this upward pressure catapults you up the ladder of success faster than you had anticipated. It's the slingshot effect. And it doesn't take much to get you started.

If there's something you've been resolving to do right after you finish this book, don't put it off again. Just do it. Even if it's something small—ordering a college catalog, updating your resume, writing a letter of inquiry, asking someone for business advice. Whatever it is, just do it. Feel the small satisfaction of getting it done. Experience the sense of completion, then go on and do the next thing. And the next. And the next. Start a pattern. Form a habit. Use the Secret.

At first, only you will notice a change. After a while, those closest to you will notice. Before you realize it, everyone will notice. By that time, your pattern of success will have become unconscious. You'll easily do things that once kept you frozen and frustrated. Instead of broken promises and halfhearted resolutions, you'll have a list of accomplishments to point to with pride. Instead of excuses and rationalizations to bore people with, you'll have interesting stories of how you got things done. Instead of a litany of unrealized dreams, your life will have become a real-life tale of dreams come true.

When we use the Forgotten Secret, we take a life of failure and unfulfilled promise and turn it into an exciting adventure. And if we can do that, what more could we possibly want?